ANGLERFISH

The Seadevil of the Deep

Elaine M. Alexander

ILLUSTRATED BY Fiona Fogg

CANDLEWICK PRESS

Far, far below the ocean's surface, where no trace of
sunlight can reach, Anglerfish makes her home.

She glides slowly through the dark water, always
on the hunt. Her jaw protrudes, baring razor-sharp
teeth. She is a fearsome creature. She is the Seadevil
of the Deep.

Anglerfish did not always reside in shadow. Her life began as a tiny egg on the surface of the Atlantic Ocean. As a baby fish, or fry, she floated gently in the light and feasted on plankton.

Near the surface, danger lurked everywhere.

Fishing nets and hungry predators prowled the waters.

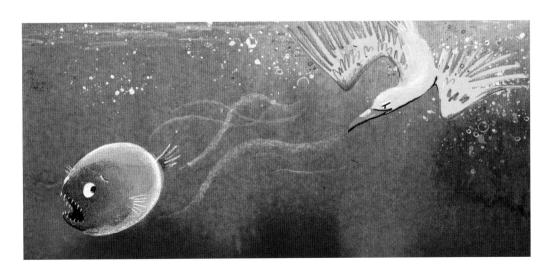

One, two, three years passed. Anglerfish grew.

Her torso rounded and her fins lengthened. When her fishing rod sprouted
from her forehead, Anglerfish began her descent into deeper water.

Halfway there, where streaks of sunlight still teased their way through the gray-green ocean, Anglerfish wobbled in the water. Her cousin Monkfish swept by.

Monkfish's broad brown-green body glistened,
and his mouth gaped in the murky sea.

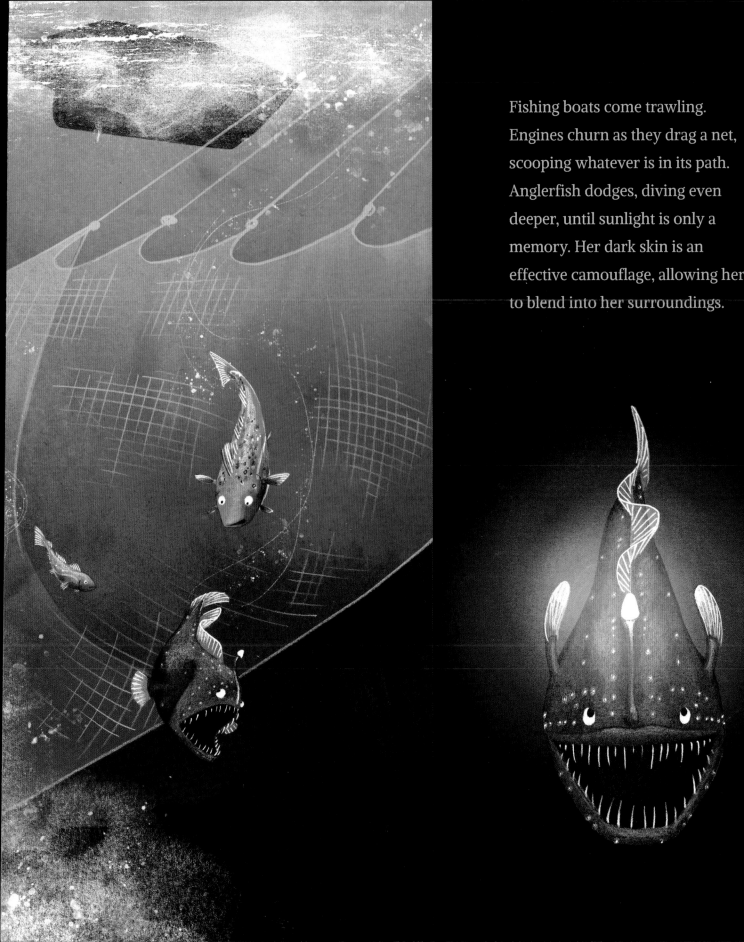

Fishing boats come trawling. Engines churn as they drag a net, scooping whatever is in its path. Anglerfish dodges, diving even deeper, until sunlight is only a memory. Her dark skin is an effective camouflage, allowing her to blend into her surroundings.

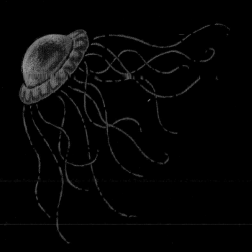

Dark as midnight, Anglerfish makes her own light. A tiny
bioluminescent lure glows at the tip of a thin, pointed fin
that grows between her eyes. She glides alone—fierce,
hungry, patient.

With a waggle of her tail, she's buried in mud and sand,
dangling the glowing orb like her very own fishing pole.
Anglerfish waits for a fish, a shrimp, or maybe even a
crab to take the bait.

Shadows shift. She wiggles her lure, hoping prey will mistake her light for a tasty morsel.

A crab shuffles closer. Anglerfish's stomach distends. Her flexible jaw extends.

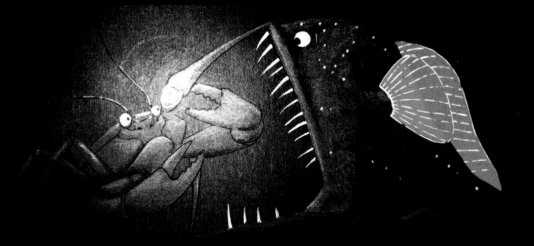

She swallows her meal whole. It's only a morsel, but food is scarce
in the midnight zone, and Anglerfish can't afford to be picky.

17

The cloud of sand settles. Anglerfish isn't
alone anymore. A tiny male anglerfish
circles, homing in on her back.

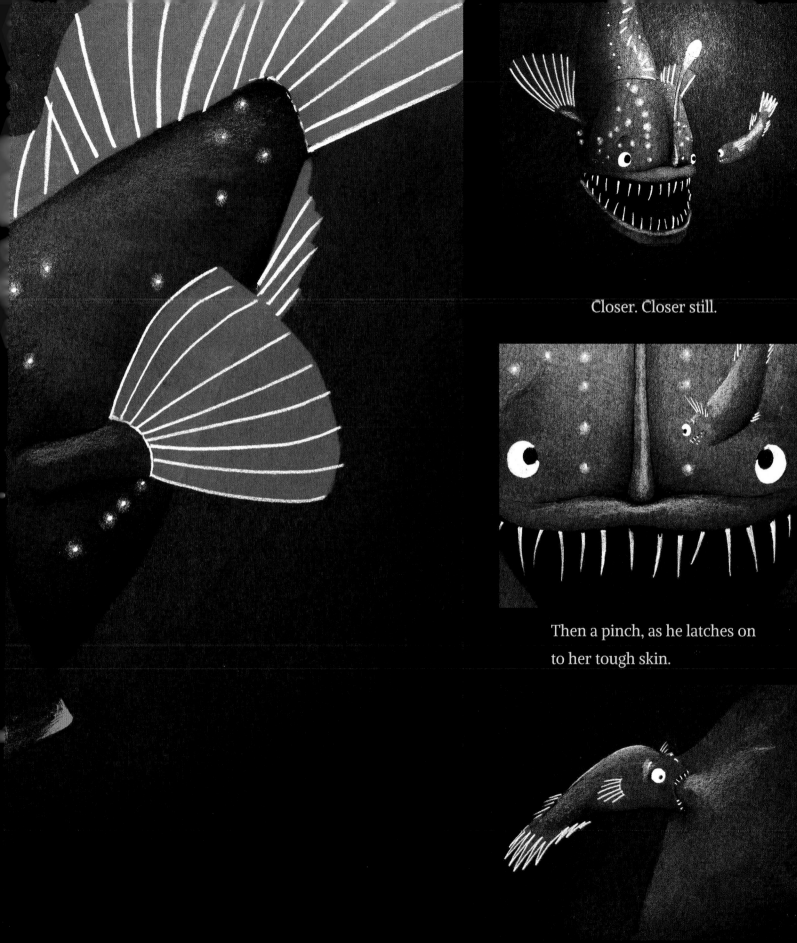

Closer. Closer still.

Then a pinch, as he latches on
to her tough skin.

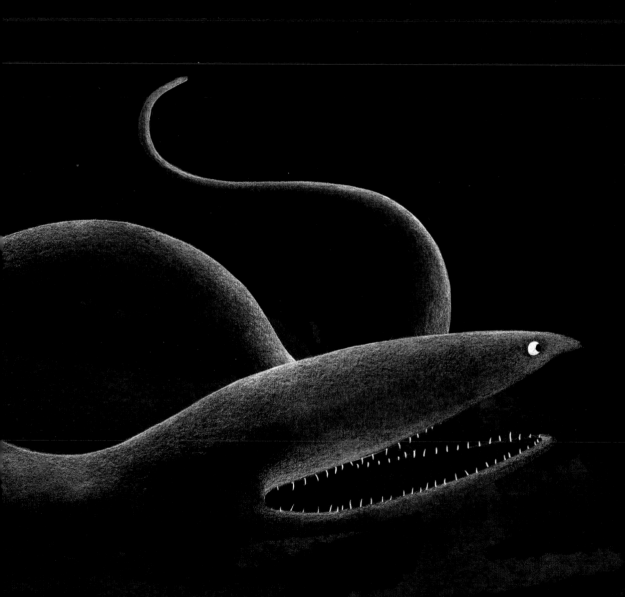

With a flick of her tail, Anglerfish swims on, carrying
the tiny male's body through the dark. A stowaway on
her solitary journey, he is being absorbed into her body.
Anglerfish will carry him with her always. Theirs is a
union necessary for survival.

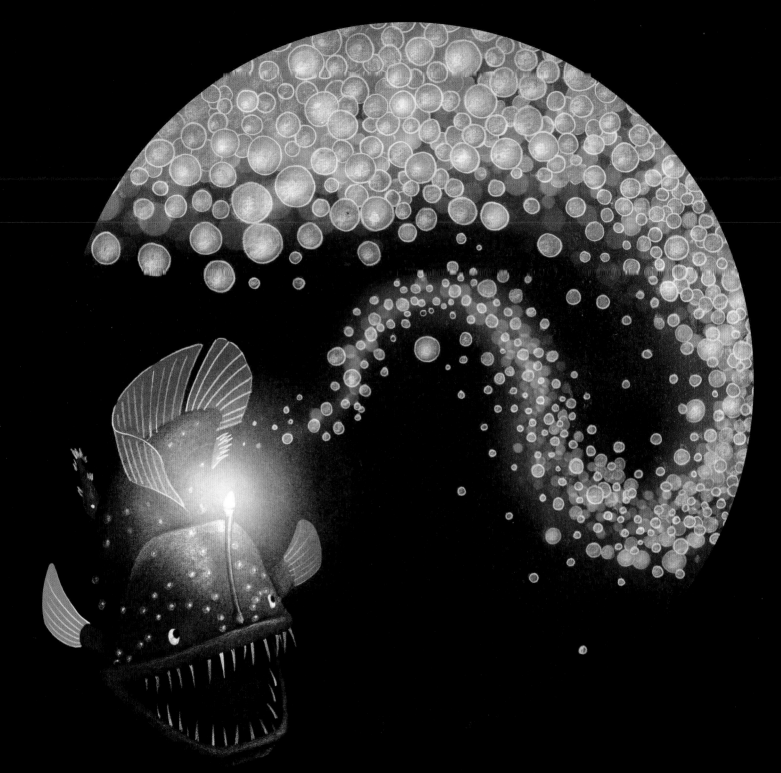

Anglerfish is ready now. Her most important work begins.
She releases fertilized eggs, too many to count. They stick
together; a thin protective gel binds them on their journey.

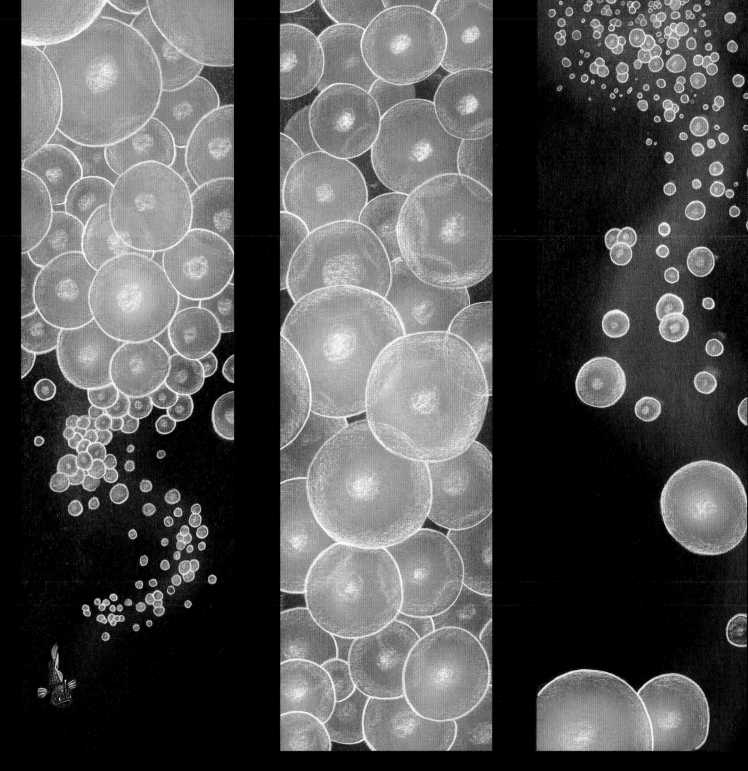

The massive spawn rises up through the ocean, higher and higher, until it is out of sight.

Far, far below the ocean's surface, where no trace of sunlight can reach, in the darkest, most sparsely inhabited place in the sea, Anglerfish is alone again.

MORE ABOUT ANGLERFISH

LIFE CYCLE AMID
THE OCEAN ZONES

Anglerfish begin their lives as tiny eggs that are released deep in the ocean and float gently to the surface. The baby fish feast on plankton. As they grow into adulthood, they begin their descent to a depth of 3,300 to 13,000 feet (1,000 to 4,000 meters) below the surface, which is called the bathypelagic zone.

Unlike some related species, such as monkfish, goosefish, or frogfish, which live in more shallow water, a mere 300 feet (90 meters) down, anglerfish mostly live thousands of feet below the surface.

Sunlight does not penetrate to that depth; it is always as dark as a starless, moonless night. In fact, that depth is called the midnight zone. Life in this part of the ocean is an isolated existence with scarce resources.

On their descent, anglerfish do live briefly in depths where some sunlight penetrates. These distances make up the mesopelagic zone, also known as the twilight zone.

Sunlight zone
650 feet (200 meters)

Twilight (mesopelagic) zone
3,000 feet (1,000 meters)

ADAPTATIONS

Some species that live in deep ocean zones, where there is scant or no light, have evolved large eyes. Some, like female anglerfish, have the ability to make their own light.

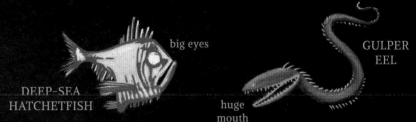

big eyes

GULPER EEL

DEEP-SEA HATCHETFISH

huge mouth

Bioluminescence is the generation and emission of light by an organism; the term is derived from Latin words for "living" and "light." Organisms with bioluminescent adaptations usually live in places where it is extremely dark.

VIPERFISH

FANFIN ANGLERFISH

They might use their light as a signal, to scare away predators, or to illuminate prey. Female anglerfish also use their glowing orb as bait, dangling it in front of their body to draw prey right to their mouth.

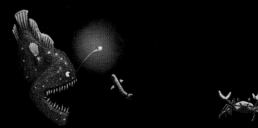

HUNTING

Anglerfish, dubbed the Seadevils of the Deep for their gaping jaws and razor-sharp teeth, are always on the hunt. These deep-sea dwellers look like throwbacks from prehistoric times, but their adaptations are well suited to survival in the ocean's depths.

Their dark skin, sometimes covered in spines and warts, allows them to blend into their surroundings.

Any organism that an anglerfish lures close suddenly finds itself trapped like a prisoner in a cell. Anglerfish jaws work like spring hinges, snapping closed quickly as the fish swallows its prey whole.

Since meals can be scarce, an anglerfish can expand her stomach to swallow organisms twice her size.

MATES

In the past, biologists mistook male anglerfish for parasites living under the skin of females. Now they know that a male attaches to a female and becomes absorbed into her body.

female   male

BLACK SEADEVIL
(*Linophryne bicornis*)

Female anglerfish vary in size from 6 inches to 3 feet (15 to 90 centimeters) long, depending on the species, while males are comparatively tiny, averaging 2½ to 6 inches (6 to 15 centimeters) long.

The union is a matter of survival. Mature males lack a digestive system and cannot survive alone. They use their keen sense of smell to seek out a healthy female, then attach to her by biting into her flesh. Once the male is attached, his jaws are dissolved by enzymes and his blood fuses with the female's. A female anglerfish may carry several males.

When the female is ready to reproduce, in the spring or early summer, an attached male fertilizes her eggs. She can lay more than a million eggs in a single spawning.

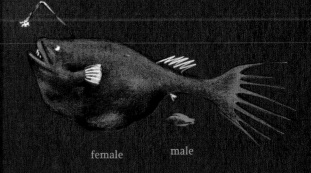

female   male

KRØYERS DEEP-SEA ANGLERFISH
(*Ceratias holboelli*)

GLOSSARY

adaptation: a trait that has developed to help an animal survive in its environment

enzymes: molecules that accelerate, or speed up, chemical reactions

parasite: an organism that must live on or in another organism (a host) to survive

plankton: tiny living organisms that float in the ocean and other bodies of water

spawn: eggs released by aquatic animals

translucent: clear, allowing light to pass through

OTHER SPECIES OF ANGLERFISH

FROGFISH

GOOSEFISH

RED-LIPPED BATFISH

OTHER SEADEVILS

FANFIN SEADEVIL

PRICKLY SEADEVIL

FOOTBALLFISH

WOLFTRAP SEADEVIL

TRIPLEWART SEADEVIL

WHIPNOSE SEADEVIL

INDEX

For the fearsome women who encouraged me to keep swimming:
Louise, Tracy, Kristen, Susan, Karen, Maryann, and Jo
EMA

For Yvonne, Peter, and Simon
FF

First edition 2022

Library of Congress Catalog Card Number 2021947159
ISBN 978-1-5362-1396-6

24 25 26 27 28 29 CCP 10 9 8 7 6 5 4 3

Printed in Shenzhen, Guangdong, China

This book was typeset in Alike Angular.
The illustrations were created digitally.

Candlewick Press
99 Dover Street
Somerville, Massachusetts 02144

www.candlewick.com